Contents

Introduction 3

Living in the "In-between" Time 5
(Isaiah 2:1-5; Romans 13:11-14; Matthew 24:36-44)

A World Turned Upside Down 15
(Isaiah 11:1-10; Romans 15:4-13; Matthew 3:1-12)

Signs of Transformation 25
(Isaiah 35:1-10; James 5:7-10; Matthew 11:2-11)

Signs of the Savior 35
(Isaiah 7:10-16; Romans 1:1-7; Matthew 1:18-25)

The Faithful Response 45
(Isaiah 9:2-7; Titus 2:11-14; Luke 2:1-20)

Meet the Writer .... **Inside Back Cover**

Cover photo: *Annunciation to the Shepherds*, by Jan Joest, 1515; PictureNow!

Introduction

Several blocks from my home is a park that is decorated for Christmas each year. An amazing number of lights are strung on each tree, bush, and flagpole. Near the center of the park is a stable with figures of Mary, Joseph, and the baby Jesus surrounded by shepherds, wise men, and assorted animals.

I have one major difficulty with this display. From Main Street, it looks like Santa and his reindeer are flying right over the top of the manger. Some have suggested to me that I should be happy that at least there is a manger.

What I see, however, is a symbol of what has happened to the celebration of the birth of Jesus. Jesus has not been completely removed from the picture, but he is sometimes hard to find and is often given a subordinate role to all the other events and routines that surround this holiday. Our youngest children can sing all of "Jingle Bells" and "Santa Clause Is Coming to Town," but they don't know "Away in a Manger" or "Silent Night." The yearly office Christmas party can be a wonderful gathering, but the celebration of Christ's birth is far from most people's minds. Television is inundated with advertising the latest items on everyone's "must-have" list, but the thought of God's generous gift of Jesus Christ is seldom mentioned. Christians often complain about losing Christ in Christmas, but this makes our preparation in the season of Advent even more important. Advent is the time for all who would follow Jesus to rekindle faith, to recall how God's promises have been fulfilled, and to renew the hope that in Christ all things can be made new. As people of faith we need to look within the Scriptures and within our hearts and affirm what the Baby in the manger means to us. The biblical readings also call us to consider what it means to look forward to the hope of Christ's coming again to judge and to establish the realm of God.

In a world that has a difficult time finding Jesus amidst shopping, parties, decorating, baking, and the many other activities that fill our calendars, Advent is the season when we are able to recall how Jesus Christ has changed our lives and will change the world. It is a time when we can hear anew the Scriptures of hope from the prophets and the promise of a new day in the words of Jesus. This is an opportunity for reaffirming that even with the commercialization of this sacred time of the year, that God in Christ can truly transform and restore our world. This season allows us to step back and reflect on the greatest gift of all, the most profound gift of love: God's presence with us in and through Jesus Christ.

Advent also is a season of invitation. Faithful followers of Jesus can share with others the hope that they find in Jesus. We need to invite all who seek hope to join us on the journey to Bethlehem, to kneel at the manger and worship the newborn King, and look forward to the promise that Christ will come again. Inviting others to find hope in Christ is difficult in the cacophony of the sights and sounds of a commercialized season, but this very cacophony indicates the need to hear and see the truth of God's love in the midst of a society that seeks love in possessions and social status.

Advent is a time to explore the Scriptures to discover what God has done for us historically, what God does in our own lives, and what God will continue to do in our future. It is a time to discern God's direction for our lives. As we read of God's faithfulness to the covenant people, we can think about our faithfulness to loving God and our neighbor, to loving and praying for our enemies, to lifting up those who are in need. In hearing the words of hope that are so prevalent in the Advent Scriptures, we can examine the ways in which we reflect hope in God when others around us place their hope in such things as power, wealth, and status.

The journey of self-examination is not always easy. However, as we reflect on the Scriptures, we are assured that God will be with us in this journey, as God has been with us all along. As we live our lives according to the teaching and example of Jesus Christ—loving others as he loved us, being willing to surrender our lives to the will of God rather than our own wills—we are able to let his light shine through us into a world that is often stuck in the shadows.

During the season of Advent, the light will shine through us as we affirm God's love for us in Christ, as we commit ourselves to helping those in need, not just in this season, but throughout the year. The light of Christ shines through us when we make worship and study in this season our first priority rather than something that is squeezed into the schedule between parties, shopping, and decorating. The light of Christ is visible to others when we do not allow the hectic pace of the season to overwhelm us but rather display the confidence and assurance that comes from experiencing God's peace. When we get to the celebration of Christmas and we feel enthusiastic about the celebration of the birth of the Savior rather than relieved that the season is over, we are letting Christ's light shine through us.

The lights strung on Christmas trees and other decorations shine brightly, but the light of Christ shines even more brightly. During the season of Advent our anticipation and preparation for the coming of Christ into our world, as infant and as King, become the light of Christ for others.

Living in the "In-between" Time

Scriptures for Advent: The First Sunday
Isaiah 2:1-5
Romans 13:11-14
Matthew 24:36-44

Advent is a time in which we anticipate and prepare for Christmas. The question is, What do we anticipate? The word *advent* itself means "coming." Within the contemporary church, Advent has become a time of preparing for the celebration of the birth of Jesus, a practice that looks to the past fulfillment of God's promises. It has only been in relatively modern times, however, that Advent became primarily a preparation for celebrating the birth of Jesus. When we look only to the past, little expectation remains. Is our anticipation of the birth of Jesus simply the act of remembering the hope of the past?

Looking back can be nostalgic, and it may instill a sense of confidence that God keeps promises. During the time that Jesus was born, some believed that God would send a special agent, an anointed leader or messiah, who would end Roman oppression and re-establish the realm of God. Others thought of the messiah as the apocalyptic Son of Man who would reign and judge for eternity. Many Christians look back to the birth of Jesus as God's fulfillment of the promise to send such a messiah and have expanded ideas about the work of the messiah beyond the specific religious and political contexts that existed in the time of Jesus.

Living in God's kingdom means living God's way of life: a way of justice, peace, and mercy for all nations. However, many of the practices and traditions surrounding the birth of Jesus do not inspire the same deeply felt hope that was expressed by those who longed for the messiah in ancient times. The modern reader might understand the hope of the Israelites of old, but what about the hope for a better world today? We need only look at the world around us to see that the kingdom of God that Jesus came to announce and initiate has not been fully realized. We need to do more in Advent than simply recount the old, old story.

In contrast to the contemporary focus on celebrating the birth of Jesus, Advent has traditionally been observed as a time of hopeful anticipation for the second coming of Christ. The Scriptures of the season address this theme of Christ's coming—or in Greek, the Parousia, which means "presence" or "arrival." In Christian usage, it refers to the time when Christ will return to usher in the kingdom of God and to judge the world according to the ways of God.

Much has been written about the Second Coming. It has become something of a cottage industry to examine the Scriptures for clues that predict the date and time of the Savior's return. All of this is to no avail, for the Scriptures clearly indicate that the fulfillment of this age will come in God's time. Mark 9:1 suggests that the time was imminent. "And he said to them, 'Truly I tell you, there are some standing here who will not taste death until they see that the kingdom of God has come with power.' " Mark 13:32-33 says that no one knows when the fulfillment of God's kingdom will occur: "But about that day or hour no one knows, neither the angels in heaven, nor the Son, but only the Father. Beware, keep alert; for you do not know when the time will come."

While looking back with gratitude at promises fulfilled, we look forward with anticipation to the promises God will fulfill in our midst. As we look to the promise of Christ's return, we can have the same kind of hope and expectation that the ancient people had as they looked towards the first coming of the messiah.

How are contemporary Christians to live between past fulfillments and the future hopes? The answers are in the biblical story. Christians have lived in an in-between time for 2,000 years, which often contrasts to our contemporary cultural focus on the present moment. The people of God are not called to live according to the culture but according to the ways of God. We look to the Scriptures of this season and reflect upon them in order to consider how our stories connect with the great story of God's grace-filled plan.

BETWEEN PERIL AND HOPE
Isaiah 2:1-5

Isaiah of Jerusalem brought the word of God to the people of Judah in the later half of the eighth century B.C. The Assyrian Empire, the great power to the north, threatened the safety and security of Israel and Judah. Into this perilous situation, Isaiah prophesied. The first 39 chapters of the Book of Isaiah record the period in time prior to the fall of the ten northern tribes of Israel.

Centuries earlier, David was able to establish a united monarchy in which all the tribes were brought under his kingship. After the death of Solomon in 922 B.C, the tribes separated again. The southern tribes of Judah and Benjamin accepted Solomon's son Rehoboam as king. When Rehoboam attempted to assert authority over the ten tribes to the north, they resisted and established their own monarchy with Jeroboam as their king. During the time that Isaiah prophesied, the people of Jerusalem looked to their neighbors to the north, who were being threatened with annihilation.

The threat of Assyria produced great fear among the people of Jerusalem. This was not only their capital city but also their center for worship. The temple built by Solomon was located in Jerusalem. God's covenant with David that he and his ancestors would forever sit on the throne provided a sense of security to the people. This was the context into which Isaiah brought the word of God.

The prophecies of Isaiah seem foreboding and frightening. The threat of the Assyrian army was real, and the future was uncertain. However, the prophet also looked ahead with a sense of expectant hope, as in the first verses of the second chapter. He instructed the nation to look beyond the immediate threat of the Assyrians to a time of peace, a time when the nations of the world will look to Jerusalem as a model for right living. Though oriented toward the future, these prophecies also recall the past promises that God had made to Abraham, Moses, and David. God had not abandoned the covenants of the past. Isaiah's words hold the past and the future in a creative tension for the people of Jerusalem.

The vision of the future that the prophet proclaimed was radically different from the vision of an Assyrian invasion. In God's call in Genesis 12, it is clear that Abraham and his descendants are blessed by God to be a blessing: "In you all the families of the earth shall be blessed" (Genesis 12:3). God's covenant with Moses provided a framework that the people might live together in peace and with a sense of order, recalled God's deliverance, and clearly established that the covenant originated with God. "I am the LORD your God, who brought you out of the land of Egypt, out of the house of slavery" (Exodus 20:2). The promise to the descendants of David was for "peace from the LORD forevermore" (1 Kings 2:33).

The image of nations uniting under the word of God and laying down weapons in favor of peace may have seemed foolhardy to a nation threatened by an advancing army. The images may seem foolhardy to contemporary Christians in the United States who feel the necessity for a mighty army that will stand against foreign powers. The call behind the images of peace is radical obedience to the ways of God. The people were tempted to mistrust that God would work in their midst. They had placed their hopes in great armies and political alliances. They had trusted their own abilities and judgments rather than the power of God to rule in their midst.

Isaiah called the people to a radically new future that would fulfill what was promised and envisioned in their past. Though this passage does not point specifically to a messianic expectation, it does point to a new age. Other portions of Isaiah's prophecy will address the messianic expectation. Isaiah opens his oracle with an image of a new kind of kingdom, one that is reflected in the words of other prophets such as Joel and Micah. It will be a kingdom of justice and mercy, where God's love will rule over all nations.

This is a fitting passage to be read at the beginning of Advent, the beginning of the liturgical year for Christians. Advent is a time for looking forward with expectation, much like the people of Israel and Judah did, at the vision God holds for the world. These first verses of Isaiah 2 begin to paint the picture of God's purpose for the people of Israel and their place within the world. The peaceful kingdom was to be transformational for all the nations of the world. When the nations looked to the holy city of Jerusalem, they would witness an obedient, faithful people governed by God's word in the Torah. The kingdom of Isaiah's prophecy would draw all the nations of the world to it, for it would be the model of justice and peace. The word of the Lord would be the measuring rod of judgment.

Christians tend to view the prophetic word of Isaiah as a mere prelude to the coming of Jesus Christ and often do not fully appreciate that the promises of God were a continual part of the history of God's chosen people. The prophets were calling the people to look to the promises of God. The people could trust in the covenants of God, who was faithful in spite of the disobedience of the people. God's purposes would be fulfilled, and God's word could be trusted as the sufficient rule for all the nations of the world. Just as God had been their hope and deliverer in the past, the time was coming when God would deliver them once again and restore them as the light to the nations.

The words of Isaiah express confidence in God's future action, an anticipation that the will of God would come to fulfillment. The impending perils with which contemporary culture lives often clouds the confidence that even faithful, church-attending Christians have in God. So many people live in fear. The disagreements among nations, communities, families, and individuals seem too great to overcome. These concerns are often mentioned in prayer but without the confidence that God will truly act. Such prayers are wishes rather than confident hope because we lack the faith that the will of God will be fulfilled in our midst. We pray wishing for a miracle, rather than praying with the hope and confidence of knowing that the power of God is greater than the powers that surround us.

The word of the prophet is needed as much now as it was needed then. None of the perils that we now encounter are more powerful than God. Advent is the season that teaches the church how to embrace the powerful vision that God offers to the world. Because God is with us in the time between the present perils and the future hope, the faithful are called to be a people of prayer, confident that God is in control. People of faith can advocate for the poor and oppressed and work toward the just world to which God has called us. God calls us to embrace peace in our lives, our families, and our communities. We are called to be peacemakers.

How do you think Isaiah 2:1-5 addresses the contemporary situation in our world? How do the words challenge you? offer you hope? What can you do to be a peacemaker in your home, church, community, and world? What might you and your church do to bring about God's peaceable kingdom?

BETWEEN THE NIGHT AND DAY
Romans 13:11-14

In Paul's letter to the church in Rome, he writes to them of living in the time between the night and the day, when dawn is about to break. He uses this metaphor to help these fledgling Christians to understand their responsibility for righteous living in the midst of their current situation, which was life lived under Roman domination. For the early church, this was the time between the resurrection/ascension of Jesus Christ and his coming again in glory. It was the expectation of the early church that Christ's return would be imminent. Paul's concern was how Christians should live in the light of Christ's life in the past as they anticipated his return in the near future. The anticipation of Christ's return provided hope for living in an uncertain present.

The church to which Paul wrote in Rome was caught in a debate between Jewish and Gentile Christians. In many of the Christian communities of faith in which Gentile Christians were present, there were questions regarding the place of Torah in daily life. Jewish Christians believed they should remain faithful to the covenant. The majority of Gentile Christians, however, did not feel bound by the Jewish law. Who, then, were the rightful heirs of Abraham and Sarah, the people chosen to be the light to the nations? In addition, the political situation fueled the fires of misunderstanding and division. The Roman emperor Claudius had banished the Jews from Rome; however, Nero rescinded this order upon his taking power in A.D. 54.

Paul called the Christians in Rome to rise above the divisions and to find unity in the good news of Jesus Christ. The quarreling and jealousy of the community was to be put aside. The moral behaviors of the community of faith needed to be above reproach, an example to the non-believers in Rome. Their actions needed to reflect the faith that they professed, not simply because the city of Rome needed a positive example, but because the time was drawing near for Christ's return. While Paul wrote that salvation is by faith and faith alone, he taught that the actions of the faithful are a reflection of their faithfulness to God.

Though he had never visited the church in Rome, it was an important community of faith because it was at the center of the empire. Rome was the political center of the empire and was the seat of its government. It was also a religious center, filled with a variety of temples to various gods known throughout the Roman world. In the Mediterranean world, all eyes looked to Rome. This gave the church in Rome not only a unique responsibility but also a unique opportunity to proclaim faithfully God's plan for the world, to exhibit how God's kingdom that Jesus announced would be realized in the practicalities of the present moment. The full realization of the kingdom of God had not yet occurred. However, this was the hope and expectation of the church, and with the belief of Jesus' imminent return, there was an anticipation that was palpable among the early Christian leaders.

The hope and expectation of an imminent return of Christ fueled a sense of urgency for Paul and other leaders of the church to spread the gospel to the ends of the earth so that all might be ready to receive Christ. Until Christ returned, Paul was advising the Christians of Rome to live each day as God intends, a way of life made known through the teaching and example of Jesus: "Put on the Lord Jesus Christ, and make no provision for the flesh" (verse 14). In other words, Paul encouraged the believers in Rome to live as Christ taught instead of following their own desires or adhering to the culture in which they were living. Only by living as Christ lived could they prepare for Christ's return, for the faithfulness of the people was all that God required. There were no other requirements and no other measures.

In the season of Advent, anticipation is a major theme. Paul encouraged the Romans to wait expectantly for the return of Christ by living an honorable life in which they loved their neighbor as themselves and thus fulfilled the law. Paul told them to "put on the armor of light." Early Christians were often referred to as children of the light, recounting the imagery of Christ as the light of the world. Paul encouraged the followers of Christ to be the light that the world needs. (See also

Matthew 5:14.) By putting on the armor of light, Christians will not only be an example but will also have the protection of Christ against the influences of the world and the enticements of seeking only personal pleasure. The journey into faithfulness includes Christ as companion and advocate, teacher and savior.

Waiting with anticipation for the Second Coming is a matter of living each day according to the ways of Christ. It is living within the demands of the great commandment to love God and to love others as oneself. To live as Christ lived is to allow this commandment to be the rudder for all our actions and ethical decisions. Such living in the present demonstrates faithful response to teachings and examples of the past shown in Jesus and the promised hope of a glorious future in Christ's return. The second advent of Christ is nothing to be feared by the faithful, for those who live with Christ await expectantly the return of their Lord.

As Christians, we tend to believe that we must earn our way into God's righteous kingdom. Advent, however, is a time in which we can acknowledge that our hope is in Christ alone and not in our own goodness or resolve. By reaffirming our faith, by examining ourselves and putting ourselves right with God, we demonstrate that God is at work through Christ in our lives. By our example, we share the good news that faith in Christ is sufficient and that by trusting in God's promises of salvation in Christ, we wait with joy and hope for Christ to come again. A bumper sticker appeared several years ago that stated, "Christ is coming again! Look busy!"

We look busy when we act in ways that will bring us the attention of others or when we do the church work without experiencing the transforming power of Christ in our lives. Our prayer becomes all talking without listening. Our church work becomes a 24/7 series of activities that lack outreach to the community and to the world. We neglect personal and communal sabbath in which we rest in the revitalizing presence of God.

The world was not prepared to receive the Christ Child 2,000 years ago, but that need not be the case for the world today. We know the light of the world, even if it is an imperfect understanding, a dim shadow of the glory that will be revealed in all its fullness when Christ returns. As people in between the time of Jesus' ascension and his coming again, Christians are called to hope and life in Jesus Christ that takes the shape of faithful living and moral uprightness. By sharing the love of God, encouraging one another, and bearing one another's burdens, we make the kingdom of God visible in our world while we await Christ's coming.

How well does your daily life exhibit your faith in Jesus Christ?

How can your actions demonstrate that you wait with hope and expectancy for our Lord? How might your actions draw others closer to the kingdom that God has promised?

BETWEEN PRESENT AND FUTURE
Matthew 24:36-44

Throughout the Gospels, there are places where Jesus speaks about the future. These passages are referred to as apocalyptic, for they reflect a particular worldview concerning the future. Apocalypticism dealt with the end of the current age and the beginning of a new day, a time ushered in by a great battle between the forces of good and evil. In spite of what might initially look like defeat, the good would ultimately triumph. It was a worldview that acknowledged that suffering was real and present but would not prevail. It was a worldview grounded in hope for a future that would come from God's hands. Jesus called his followers to be alert, to watch for the signs that the time was at hand.

Jesus clearly indicates in Matthew 24:36-44 that even he was not aware of the time when the end of the age would come. This seems somewhat contradictory, for in the verses just prior to these he named events that would precede the coming of the Son of Man and that "this generation will not pass away until all these things have taken place" (verse 34). Consider his use of the example of Noah. The ark was a sign of something to come, and the preparations of Noah and his family were done faithfully in view of the entire world; but it was not until God sent the rains from the heavens that they knew the time. Jesus likened the coming of the Son of Man to the story of Noah. Faithful anticipation and preparation is necessary, but there is no way of knowing the precise moment when Christ will return. The time is in God's hands.

So how can the faithful prepare? Jesus told them to be always ready, always prepared. In Jesus' mind, the issue is not the time preceding and the circumstances surrounding the coming of God's kingdom. The issue is our faithfulness.

Jesus' use of the story of Noah raises another point. It was following the flood of Noah that God set the rainbow in the clouds, a sign of the covenant between God and Noah and with all of Noah's descendents. Covenants are signs of God's faithfulness. In recounting the story of Noah, Jesus is also reminding the people of God's faithfulness, even when God's plan may not be fully understood. By sending Jesus into the world, God showed faithfulness to the covenants. This was surely a sign for God's people. Nor would he leave them as orphans (John 14:18). He would return and bring them to be with him (John 14:3). The present and future times might not be easy; but in the midst of struggle, turmoil, and persecution, Jesus called his followers to be mindful of the covenants that God had made and that God had kept, even when the people had not been faithful.

These verses are not the only place in the Gospel where Jesus calls his followers to be always ready, to be awake. Most of Matthew 24–25 deals with the end times. Jesus came to announce and initiate the kingdom of God; he called on his followers to be diligent and faithful to the ways of God, to live each day consistent with his life and teachings. For Christians, the present moment is buoyed by a future hope. Thinking of God's tomorrow makes it possible for us to live that future today. God has acted in the past and will continue to act in the future, even when that future is not fully clear to us.

What is difficult to hear in these passages of the coming glory of Christ is the judgment that accompanies his glory. In this passage, Jesus speaks about two men in the field and two women grinding meal together. In both cases, as they do the same task, they look the same. However, in God's view, there is a difference, for one will be taken away and protected, as was Noah and his family, and the other is not. What is puzzling to the listener is that there appears to be no difference. Is God arbitrary? By no means! Jesus indicates that those who are vigilant and always ready are the ones who will be chosen. The parable of the wise and foolish maids recorded in Matthew 25 points to this teaching. The separation of the people as the farmer separates the sheep and goats points to the necessity of feeding the hungry, offering water to the thirsty, and welcoming the stranger, all of which are hallmarks of the kingdom way of life.

Doing the will of God and trusting in God's promises signal the hope and joy of the Advent season. This runs counter to cultural norms. People entrust their security to their livelihoods to institutions, their money to banks, their futures to political leaders, their security to armies. In the midst of the secular Christmas culture that surrounds the church during the season of Advent—the shopping, the parties, the frenetic pace—there is a great need to shout loudly and clearly the message that it is in God, and God alone, that we have our hope. God came to us as a man, Jesus of Nazareth, whose birth is celebrated at Christmas; and there is work to do until the Kingdom is fully realized.

As followers of Jesus Christ, we are called to share in the vision that is the kingdom of God. We find in the Beatitudes and throughout the Sermon on the Mount in Matthew 5–7 ways in which we might participate in God's kingdom. We find hope as we catch a glimpse of the kingdom that God intends for us.

Hope for Christians today lies in the same place that the faithful, chosen people of God looked in the time of Isaiah and in the time of Paul: from God and God's Messiah. In this season of Advent, few will be thinking about Christ's coming again. The displays of holiday lights that line our streets and town centers, the carols ringing from every loud speaker at the mall, the gifts and the joys of the season will lose their shine and luster within a few weeks. By the time the manger set is packed away with the rest of the decorations, Christmas will be a memory and it will be time to move on. However, if we heed the lesson of Advent that Christ is coming again, the season becomes the beginning of the excitement and anticipation of all that God will do for us in the future. Because God has been faithful to the promises of the past, we can count on God.

How has Christ provided hope for you in your life? Who do you know who needs to know the hope that only Christ can give? How will you help them to experience this hope?

A World Turned Upside Down

Scriptures for Advent: The Second Sunday
Isaiah 11:1-10
Romans 15:4-13
Matthew 3:1-12

While Advent is a time for waiting, the question that follows is, Waiting for what? The Scriptures for the season remind us that God has acted dramatically and decisively within the world through Jesus Christ. We are waiting for Christ's return when the world, as we know it, will be turned upside down, where God's kingdom will be fully realized, a time when justice will "roll down like waters, / and righteousness like an ever-flowing stream" (Amos 5:24).

Many today do not see a great need for radical redirection, for a new time and age. Such a vision of God's kingdom is radically different from life as we experience it. With the coming of the Messiah, God was beginning a transformation in which the promises of the covenant would be fulfilled and the whole created order would be restored.

Advent is a season of introspection, of looking deeply within one's heart. Like Lent, the church has historically seen Advent as a time for turning our lives Godward, which is precisely what Isaiah, Paul, and John the Baptist address. God will bring about a new day, a time that will bring harmony and peace to all. This will be a world that is re-created and restored according to God's original intent for all creation and a world that reflects the promises that God has made throughout the generations.

A NEW LEADER WILL RISE
Isaiah 11:1-10

The olive tree is an important part of the culture of ancient Israel. Many depended on the cultivation of olives for their livelihood. Olive oil was used for lights, for anointing kings and priests, for healing, for food, and for the manufacturing of soap. Its leaves remain green, with a silvery tint on the underside that does not turn brown and dry in the arid season of the year. One of the key characteristics of the olive tree is its longevity. An olive tree can be fertile and productive for 1,000 years or more. Olive trees in the garden of Gethsemane on the Mount of Olives in Jerusalem date back to the time of Jesus. The key to their longevity is an incredibly durable root system that feeds new shoots that spring up from the base of the tree. In biblical times, the shoots that grew from the base of the tree were planted to create new trees. Even a tree that has been severely cut back and that is little more than a stump can still produce new shoots.

When the people heard the prophet Isaiah speak about the shoot that would grow from the stump of Jesse, the picture of the olive tree would have been in their minds. They would imagine new sprouts springing up around what otherwise might have appeared to be a tree that had died. The strength and endurance that the olive tree represented and symbolized was for them a sign of hope, comfort, and strength. As they looked from Jerusalem to their neighbors in the north, they were aware of the advancing Assyrian army. The threat of annihilation at the hands of this super power was a real fear. Where was their hope? Who would rise up to lead them against the enemy?

Isaiah of Jerusalem brought them the message of hope. God would raise up for them a new leader from the house of David. In times of uncertainty, people often look back to a time that seems to them to be the "good old days" for steadfast assurance. The people looked to the time of David, the great king, who united the tribes of Israel, who defeated powerful enemies, and who established Jerusalem as their capital and holy city. God had made a covenant with David that his line would sit on the throne for the people throughout the generations. The people of Jerusalem were looking for assurance that God had not abandoned the covenants. Their hope was in a renewed and strengthened bond that would persevere, even if it did not seem that way at the time. Renewal and life would spring up like the roots of the olive trees that were such an essential part of their daily lives.

David was more than just a great leader. He was the personification of the nation. He was the youngest of Jesse's son, a mere shepherd, who faced down the giant Philistine Goliath. David was chosen by God and anointed by God's prophet Samuel to lead the nation. He was not a likely choice to be a great leader, yet God raised him up for this great purpose.

Isaiah 42:6 reminded the people that they were chosen by God to be a light to the nations. They were chosen to be the ones who would live according to the ways of God, and nations would be judged according to their standard. Of course, David, like those who heard Isaiah's words, did not fully live up to God's great purpose. God, however, remained faithful to the covenant with them. This was a sign of hope for the nation, who, in spite of their unfaithfulness, knew God as steadfast and loving.

The people needed a new leader, one raised by God to lead the nation into a new age. This new leader would usher in a time in which the entire created order would find itself dwelling in harmony. Wolves and lambs would live together, children could handle snakes without fear. Those who had been natural enemies would live together in peace. Knowledge of the Lord would prevent all hurt and destruction. The world as they knew it would be turned upside down.

The new Kingdom envisioned in the words of Isaiah's prophecies is a kingdom of peace, where the oppressed, the poor, and the meek find justice, where righteousness is the measure of all people. The new Kingdom is a vision of hope for a nation that was watching their sister nation to the north being conquered and dragged off into exile. Was there any hope of escape from this worldly power? Isaiah reminded them that their hope was in the Lord who had made covenant with David and his line, who was faithful to the covenant at all times, and who would lead them into a new time unlike anything they had known.

The temptation for the leaders of Judah was to take matters into their own hands and usher in the Kingdom by looking for alliances with neighboring powers. Isaiah warned them that their hope did not lie in military powers like Egypt or Mesopotamia. Any kingdom established by strife and war would continue to be filled with strife and warring with other nations. The peaceful Kingdom that Isaiah presents can only come from an alliance with God and God's anointed leader, a Child born who would be called Wonderful Counselor, Mighty God, Everlasting Father, Prince of Peace (Isaiah 9:6).

It is uncertain whom Isaiah had in mind as he delivered these words, although Christians would later identify this anointed leader of God as Jesus Christ. There is no internal evidence within the Book of Isaiah itself nor in the historical records of the Old Testament as to whom Isaiah is talking about. What is clear is that there was a need among the people for words of hope, for a promise that moved beyond the present moment and offered hope to future generations. Like the olive tree that bears its fruit for centuries, the kingdom that would spring forth could not be cut down by military powers. The vision of a new kingdom was empowered by the eternal Spirit of God.

In the season of Advent, the church looks for the hope that comes from God in Jesus Christ. The work of the Kingdom arrived in our midst in Jesus Christ, yet wars persist and people are oppressed. Inequity between nations and within nations is a reality. Hungry and homeless people walk the streets of our cities. The vision of a created order in which people and all creation live together in harmony has not been fully realized. The culture in which we live places its hope in a rising stock market, in powerful military force, in international treaties, in legislation of laws, in medical breakthroughs, in intellectual prowess. Our society looks to its political leaders, its medical pioneers, or its scientists to create a vision of a new world where there is peace and wholeness. As we recognize such realities during Advent, the church declares that God is the source for fulfilling this vision.

Hope is rekindled when people find healing and wholeness, when the people of God reach out to offer compassion and love in a difficult, painful world. While some might believe that this new Kingdom can only come through human endeavor, the real hope lies in God who has cast the vision for us and provides the gifts so that the world that we know can be turned upside down.

What would God's kingdom look like in today's context? Isaiah spoke of an olive tree as a symbol. What would be an appropriate symbol from contemporary culture that would help others to glimpse what God's peaceful kingdom is like?

GOD IS ALWAYS FAITHFUL
Romans 15:4-13

Did God abandon the covenant with the descendents of Abraham with the advent of the Messiah, Jesus Christ? This question was at the heart of one of the earliest tensions within the church, a conflict that Paul addressed in a number of the communities of faith to which he wrote. In Rome, the capital city of the empire, the tensions between Jewish and Gentile Christians were particularly troublesome. Paul was also sensitive to the anti-Judaism that existed in Rome and, quite possibly, among Gentile Christians who lived in Rome.

Claudius expelled Jews from Rome in A.D. 49, and Paul's friends Prisca and Aquila had been among those expelled (Acts 18:2). As Paul brought his long letter to the Romans to a conclusion, he encouraged unity and harmony and recalled the words of Isaiah to demonstrate God's faithfulness as seen in Jesus Christ. "The root of Jesse shall come, / the one who rises to rule the Gentiles; / in him the Gentiles shall hope" (Romans 15:12).

At the heart of the struggle between Jewish and Gentile Christians is the question of how to view the law of Moses and the teachings of the prophets. Was the law no longer valid? Was it ever valid? If it was not valid, how could they trust in the faithfulness of God to keep the covenants? Paul believed that in Jesus Christ, the Scriptures (what Christians call the Old Testament) are fulfilled; and therefore in Christ, God has faithfully kept the covenants with the chosen people of Israel. This is the hope for all, Jew and Gentile, as the present and future hope according to Paul. He wrote, "By steadfastness and by the encouragement of the scriptures we might have hope" (verse 4).

In Paul's view, all people, Gentiles and Jews, could fulfill their purpose of being a light to the nations by following Jesus Christ. All the world would see and know the steadfast love of God. Paul quotes Deuteronomy 32:43; Psalms 18:49; 117:1; and Isaiah 11:10 to support his view.

Paul's stated vision is for a united community all worshiping together the one Lord and Savior, Jesus Christ. All people will praise God together, "so that together you may with one voice glorify the God and Father of our Lord Jesus Christ" (Romans 15:6). Paul echoes this concern in other letters, such as when he writes to the Philippian church, "Make my joy complete: be of the same mind, having the same love, being in full accord and of one mind" (Philippians 2:2). The unity of which Paul writes is a sign that the kingdom of God, which Jesus inaugurated, is coming into being. The coming of Jesus Christ made the vision real. Paul helps the church focus on the prize of the coming time when all of God's people would live as one community of faith, as one body of Christ.

The work of the church, then and now, is to break down the dividing walls and the barriers that prevent the full realization of the kingdom of God. It is a vision cast by Paul in his letters and a vision of hope for the church today.

The hope that we focus on in Advent is not a wish list of impossibilities. Hope is grounded in the promise that can become a reality through God's grace. Hope, therefore, is a means of overcoming the fatalistic attitudes that plague our society today. Hope allows persons to trust in a better, more glorious future. Human endeavor has not moved us closer to a better world. Hope, therefore, must be in God whose promises are steadfast.

This is why it was important for Paul to address the issue of the covenant that God had made with Israel. Had God abandoned the covenant in favor of a new "chosen people," might God also abandon the church of Jesus Christ at some future point? Paul reminds the church that God has not abandoned the promises made to Abraham and his descendents. God was faithful to the covenant made with David. The history of God's faithfulness affirms that God will always remain faithful, as was demonstrated in Jesus Christ, who came that these earlier covenants might be fully realized.

Christians look forward in the season of Advent, not only to the celebration of God's fulfillment of the promises made to the people of Israel in Jesus Christ, but also a time to look forward to the promise of Christ's return. Paul had an expectation of Christ's return, although he had come to accept that the Parousia might not occur until after his death (2 Corinthians 5).

Christians have long debated just what the Second Coming will be like and have looked at the evidence of the New Testament to gain understanding. Will Christ come before or after a time of trial and tribulation? Will Christ come as a physical person or a spiritual presence? Will the faithful be taken up to heaven before the coming of Christ or after?

There is no single answer to these questions. However, the vision of what is to come is amazingly consistent: God will reign over a new time of lasting peace and harmony. The ways of God will be the rule for all people. All creation will be restored and justice shall reign.

Many people today might question whether the promise of a glorious future is a realistic possibility. Two thousand years have passed since the time of Jesus of Nazareth. Peace seems to be a distant dream as nations seek to exert power over others by violence. In an increasingly secularized world, the kingdom of God seems further and further away. What are Christians to believe, and how are they to respond to those who find Christianity irrelevant? It is even difficult to find Christ in the midst of the preparations that surround us in the season of Advent. For many people, Christ is an afterthought.

Paul's words to the Romans speak to the church today as they did in his time. God has been faithful to all of the covenants. God's word can be trusted. God encourages. His call for harmony speaks to us as it did to Jewish and Gentile Christians. Christ has come to transform the entire world: believer and unbeliever. All Christians are called to be a light to the world, to be the reminder that it is in Christ that we find harmony, hope, and peace.

"Welcome one another, therefore, just as Christ has welcomed you, for the glory of God" (Romans 15:7). We too can heed these words and welcome one another for the glory of God. In many ways, Advent is the perfect season for such welcoming, an attitude and action that shows the world the light of Christ, even though it may seem difficult when others are so preoccupied with gifts and parties and other events of the season.

For Christians, the promise of the peace of Christ is not just a future hope but can be a life-giving force in the midst of what can be a stressful season. Many struggle with loss, illness, and pain in their lives. Many have difficulty finding joy. The season of Advent provides opportunities to be the light of Christ to one another within the community of faith and to the entire world.

Where have you seen God's promises fulfilled in your life? How do these promises help you, and others, to experience the hope that is part of this season? How might you be able to share that hope with your family, your friends and neighbors, those who are not experiencing the joy of the season, and those who find God irrelevant in their lives? How might you welcome others and build harmony for the glory of God?

A CALL TO REPENTANCE
Matthew 3:1-12

The Judean wilderness is a dry, vast desert. From this wilderness came the voice of one who challenged the religious leaders 2,000 years ago. John the Baptist proclaimed that the kingdom of heaven was drawing near. The wilderness was a significant place for the children of Israel. It was in the wilderness that God called to Moses and sent him to Pharaoh (Exodus 3) and then delivered to Moses the Law that would govern the people (Exodus 20). It was in the wilderness that God's still, small voice spoke to Elijah (1 Kings 19). In Matthew 3:1-12, the voice of God resonates in a new time and circumstance in the person of John the Baptist. John's significance cannot be overlooked, as all four Gospel writers include his story as part of the prelude to Jesus' public ministry.

While the Gospel of Matthew quotes from the prophet Isaiah (Isaiah 40:3), John more closely resembled the prophet Elijah in style and demeanor. He did not shy away from being bold in his speech. John was not afraid to confront those in power, much like his model Elijah who dared to challenge King Ahab and his wife Jezebel. (See 1 Kings 21 for an example of Elijah's challenge to the king.) John seems to have aligned himself with the classical prophetic tradition that is represented by Elijah and others. By so doing, he was sending the message that the worship of the one true God and justice for the poor and the oppressed are essential.

His rough appearance and his diet of wild locusts and honey certainly separated him from those who lived in the cities and villages of Judea and Galilee. John seems to have found many ways to distance himself from other religious leaders of the day and, accordingly, was able to draw the attention of the people of Jerusalem and Judea. This was not a party-line prophet who would only bring words that would support and encourage the status quo. John the Baptist was a straight-speaking, independent-minded prophet who announced the coming of God's anointed one.

However, John had a message himself: It was a message of repentance, calling people to confess their sins and to turn their lives toward God. His message raised questions among religious leaders. The Pharisees and Sadducees, persons who held to different interpretations of the Jewish law, had heard of him and went out to the wilderness for baptism.

Archeological evidence shows that there were ritual baths around the Temple in Jerusalem and in other religious centers through Judea. This kind of ritual cleansing, therefore, was not a new phenomenon. John's baptism, however, was different. While these other symbolic cleansing rituals prepared people for participation in the religious traditions handed down to them, John's baptism signaled a complete change of one's life. It was a "baptism of repentance."

John challenged the Pharisees and Sadducees. He questioned their intentions, as if by coming for baptism they might be able to avoid the coming judgment. John knew their hearts. They depended on the faith they had inherited as their salvation. He announced to them that simply being a descendent of Abraham was not enough. God's judgment would be based on a changed heart; and a changed heart could be seen by outward actions, or "fruit worthy of repentance" (Matthew 3:9). Repentance was necessary for new life.

Though John spoke boldly of God's judgment, his primary message was of one who was to come, God's chosen one, who would be the true judge of all humankind. John uses the imagery of the wheat harvest when the farmer would toss the grain into the air and the winds would blow away the chaff while the wheat fell to the threshing floor. The one whom John is announcing is not a gentle baby lying in a manger. John is announcing one who will challenge the status quo, who will raise a new standard, who will judge with righteousness, and who will come with the power of the Holy Spirit.

In the traditional Christmas narratives, the story of the birth of John the Baptist is prominent. However, in the Advent Scriptures, the announcement of John is not tied to the birth of Jesus. It is tied to the announcement of one who will come with the authority of a judge. John calls the people who come to him in the wilderness to reform their lives in preparation for a new day that will be inaugurated with the coming of God's anointed one.

Is there still a new day coming? Many doubt that this is even a remote possibility, at least on earth. Even Christians resolve to accept life as it is with all hope focused on an eternal life in a heavenly home. Repentance is viewed as a personal process that puts the believer's heart right with God, not as an action that moves the community of faith closer to realizing God's kingdom in our midst. The extreme individualism that is so ingrained in Western society has taken hold among the people of faith; but the Christian tradition affirms the necessity of community, where the body of Christ can bring to the world the transforming good news that no individual can bring alone. It has been said that God is less concerned about our own transformation than how our lives have been used to bring transformation to others. That may be a slight overexaggeration; however, it is God's intention in the good news of Jesus Christ that the world, through him, might be saved.

What might a transformed world look like? The inequities that divide people according to economic and social status would no longer exist. The fears that arise from racial and ethnic differences would be erased, and all persons would be affirmed for who they are as uniquely gifted children of God. The concept of a dominant culture would be eliminated, for all persons would be viewed as members of the family of God. Cooperation and affirmation would replace competition. Most importantly, all persons would put God first in their lives, they would seek God's will in all that they do, and they would see themselves as instruments of God's shalom in the world.

Is such a society possible? Not if we attempt to accomplish this all by ourselves, for human failings always get in the way. However, with God's grace, with a willingness to let God rule in our lives, the promise of a transformed world "on earth as it is in heaven" is a real possibility. Even if we have not arrived, there are places where we catch a glimpse of the Kingdom. Advent is a time to examine our hearts, to commit ourselves to being under the lordship of Christ, so that God might use us to move the world closer to the vision of a new kingdom in our midst.

Prophets and apostles expressed a vision of a peaceful kingdom in which the faithful are God's instruments for a transformed world. To be effective instruments, we need to understand how God has transformed our lives. To understand our own need for repentance so that we might be more consistent with the ways of God is one important step in being transformed.

How would you help someone else understand what needs to be done to bring God's kingdom into reality? Since repentance is defined as turning your life Godward, what steps do you need to take in this season of Advent to bring yourself more in line with how God intends for us to live?

Signs of Transformation

Scriptures for Advent: The Third Sunday
Isaiah 35:1-10
James 5:7-10
Matthew 11:2-11

"It's beginning to look a lot like Christmas." So the familiar song goes. Lights and decorations, Christmas cards and parties, carols and gifts—all of them help us to know that Christmas is coming soon These are the signs that predominate in our culture. However, before the celebration of Christmas was commercialized and mass-marketed, the anticipation of Christmas had little to do with any of these visible signs. Advent remains a time for the church to focus its attention on the coming of Christ and the coming of his kingdom. Such signs are not as marketable nor are they as frivolous as those in the culture at large.

The biblical passages for the third week of Advent tell how God's transforming power is at work in our world. God's relationship with humanity calls us to new, abundant life in Jesus Christ. Isaiah described the transformation in terms of healing those who were blind or deaf.

Transformation is described as "the strengthening of the weak, of lifting up the downtrodden." It is seen in the dry desert becoming fertile with springs gushing forth. God's desire is that creation will be transformed by the power of God and that the entire world will be able to witness God's presence and power in the transformation. Certainly, the power of God is visible in Isaiah's vision.

The Letter of James argues that faith in Jesus Christ provides a visible transformation in the actions of believers. Christians are the signs of God's power to change hearts. Our lives as Christians witness to the faith that we profess. Works do not substitute for faith, but they do demonstrate the reality of faith in a person's life. Advent becomes a wonderful opportunity for Christians to analyze their actions and to ask whether their actions reflect their faith. The commercialized celebration of Christmas has little interest in the good news of Christ's coming. Nevertheless, the church remains convinced that Advent is an appropriate time for introspection, especially introspection that seeks the transformation that Christ offers.

When we experience the transformation that God offers us in Jesus Christ, our hearts are changed and the signs we look for change. Because Jesus is truly the Savior, trusting in him changes our hearts and makes our spirits whole. Unlike John the Baptist, we need not ask ourselves if Jesus really is the Christ. We know that Jesus is the Messiah, God's chosen and anointed one, because we have been touched by his power. The signs that others are looking for are present within our hearts and find expression in our actions.

ALL CREATION IS A SIGN
Isaiah 35:1-10

Biblical scholars divide the Book of Isaiah into at least two, and sometimes three, distinct sections. Isaiah 1–39 comes from an historical period prior to the fall of the northern kingdom of Israel in the latter part of the eighth century B.C. Chapters 40–55 describe the Exile in Babylon sometime after 587 B.C., and the rest of the book is placed at a time immediately following their return. Chapter 35 functions as a bridge between these two parts of the book. It echoes the imagery and language of the earlier chapters and foreshadows imagery that is to come in Chapters 40 and beyond. What makes this significant is that the message of these verses is not specifically tied to a single historical moment but reminds the reader that truly prophetic messages transcend the generations. The message of the prophet is as powerful today as it was in the time of Isaiah.

Isaiah speaks of the visible signs that God's transforming hand is at work in our world. The first sign mentioned is a transformation of the created order. The dry and barren desert will become fertile and fruitful. Waters will spring forth and there will be streams in the desert. With this image, the prophet recalls the story of Moses and the people of Israel in the wilderness at Massah and Meribah, a story in which the people argued with Moses. According to the account in Exodus 17, Moses struck the rock and water gushed forth for the people to drink. Through the miraculous hand of God, water appeared in the desert; life sprang forth where it otherwise seemed impossible.

The promised transformation is also to be seen in the healing of the sick and infirmed. The blind will see, the lame will walk, the deaf will hear. God will lift up and strengthen those who are weak. While these healing images demonstrate the compassion of God, they are significant in yet another way. One popular belief that continued to spring up throughout biblical history is the view that illness, poverty, and need are signs of divine disfavor, while health and wealth are signs of God's blessings.

Isaiah challenged this belief by describing a transformation not only of individuals who will now be well, but a transformation of the community of faith's understanding of the very nature of God. Those whom society viewed with disfavor and fear will be lifted up. God will strengthen the weak. God's favor is with those who are in need. Actually, this had always been the nature of God who lifted up the Hebrew people when they were slaves in Israel and brought them to a promised land. Similarly, God selected David, a seventh son and mere shepherd, to be the great king. Isaiah's words presented a radical change from what had been the growing understanding among the people of Jerusalem about God's favor and disfavor.

A third sign of the prophet is a highway in the desert. This imagery is used again in Isaiah 40 as words of comfort for those who are in exile. The highway will be the pathway of God by which those who are redeemed may return to the holy city of Jerusalem. Isaiah is obviously stating that in the short term the future of the people of Judah and Jerusalem will be captivity, for *redemption* is a term that signifies the buying of a slave's freedom or the buying back of the first-born in the sacrificial system found in the Torah. While redemption also had a spiritual significance, the physical description of the releasing of captives was powerful in its own right. God will rescue those in captivity; and God will provide a clear pathway whereby the faithful might return to the holy mountain of Zion, their beloved Jerusalem. The return will be marked with tremendous joy and exuberance, for these people will know that it was God who has brought them home.

In the created world, as in all the faithful children of God, the glory of the Lord shall be revealed. In the wilderness, as the Hebrew people were fleeing Egypt, the glory of the Lord appeared as a cloud or as fire. It descended upon the Tabernacle when God spoke to the people. It descended upon Mount Sinai in the wilderness as Moses ascended the mountain to speak with God. It descended upon the newly constructed Temple in Jerusalem at the time of Solomon. Isaiah also speaks of the glory of the Lord, but he does not speak in images of fire or a cloud. He uses images of vegetation and highways in the desert as the people return from exile. In these signs, the presence of God will be manifest anew. God will speak to the faithful through these signs of transformation.

Transformation of the world, of the community of faith, and

of a person can be seen by others. The dramatic transformation that the prophet describes is one in which God draws close to us and acts in human history. God's immanence is a unique claim of the Judeo-Christian tradition. In other traditions, gods were to be feared. People did pray and sacrifice to their gods, but they did not think in terms of having a relationship with them. Rather, because the gods were so fickle, they mostly wanted to keep as far away from these gods as possible. The God of the Old and New Testaments is a God who draws near and acts among us in visible ways that can be witnessed by others.

On May 18, 1980, Mount Saint Helens in Washington State erupted. The land and wildlife for miles around was destroyed, with little left but volcanic ash and massive mud slides. It was a lifeless place that scientists said would never recover. Yet, within weeks, animals that had been hibernating below the ground managed to dig their way through the ash; and within ten years, the plant life was able to again support the wildlife that had been there previously. In the words of Isaiah, "The wilderness and the dry land shall be glad, / the desert shall rejoice and blossom.... / They shall see the glory of the LORD" (Isaiah 35:1, 2). God has created an amazingly resilient world, a sign of the restorative and transforming power.

Servants of God, such as Bishop Desmond Tutu of South Africa and Archbishop Oscar Romero of El Salvador, stand as signs that God continues to call captives into freedom and those who are poor and oppressed into new life. God's concern for those who are in need transforms not just those persons but also the entire family of God.

There are still signs that God's transforming power is releasing persons from captivity. Think of persons whom Alcoholics Anonymous and other twelve-step groups have released from their addictions. Think of persons who have set aside consumerism in order to adopt lives of simplicity. Think of persons who no longer seek power and prestige in society but are satisfied with servant lifestyles. Isn't Advent a wonderful time to consider the ways God is transforming not only the world but also your life?

How do you see signs that God is present, transforming the world and people? What in your life needs to be transformed? To what are you captive? What stands in the way of allowing God's transforming power to work in your life? What are the signs that let you know God is seeking to overcome this barrier?

THE FAITHFUL ARE GOD'S SIGNS
James 5:7-10

The Letter of James was written to instruct the early Christian churches. Its opening verse addresses the twelve tribes in the Diaspora, which refers to all the faithful people spread throughout the Roman Empire. To Jewish Christians facing possible suffering and a testing of their faith, James wrote, "My brothers and sisters, whenever you face trials of any kind, consider it nothing but joy" (James 1:2). Although Martin Luther called the Letter of James "an epistle of straw," it is actually an important letter that emphasizes that genuine faith results in outward actions and responses. Faithful people can be identified by the way they treat others.

Like other New Testament writers, James expected Christ to come again and soon. In the meantime, the author instructs the faithful to be patient and to wait for that time when Christ will come and judge all the nations of the world. He also counsels them to strengthen their hearts and not to grumble at one another. It is both humbling and embarrassing to realize that from the very beginning of the church, faithful Christians have been grumbling at one another because they have grown impatient with God's timeline. James cites two examples to encourage the faithful to be patient and endure. The first is that of a farmer who knows well the workings of the world of nature. The farmer trusts that rains will water the earth, so he plants seeds and tills the soil. Anticipating the rain, the farmer waits patiently for this gift.

The other example that James uses is that of the prophet who spoke the truth of God in the midst of difficult circumstances. Because of the nature of their message, few prophets were eagerly received. Many suffered because of their prophecies, from those who heard the message and from deep within their own hearts as they agonized for their own people. Yet the prophets trusted in God and endured their suffering patiently. The Jewish Christians to whom James's letter was addressed would have been intimately familiar with the words of the prophets, for they were read and discussed in synagogues throughout the Roman Empire.

James did not speak of patience and endurance as virtues in order to build the character of those who were reading his letter. He wanted his readers to be prepared for the day of the Lord's coming, which would be a time of judgment. James called on faithful Christians to live with patience and endurance, which demonstrate trust in God's plan and in God's providence. Patience and endurance would result in an inner peace that would be visible to those who felt anxious about their future. They would serve as signs that their faith in Jesus Christ made a difference in their lives.

Does faith in Jesus Christ make a visible difference in the lives of faithful followers today? Some might argue that this is unimportant, that the only thing that matters is entering into the eternal life promised by God. James would counter that our faith should take the form of visible works so that they may be signs to others, a light to those who are living in the midst of the shadows. God utilizes the faith journey of believers to spark interest in those who have yet to hear the good news of Jesus Christ. The faith of the believer can help those who are on the margins, uncertain of what they believe, to see the blessings of Jesus Christ in their lives.

This does not mean that Christians will have an easy or perfect life. That is abundantly clear in James's letter, as he writes about suffering and endurance. Some would like to believe that if they are faithful attendees at church, if they do the right things, pray the right prayers, read the Scriptures, and live a good life that they will be exempt from disease, stress, pain, and suffering. God nowhere makes this promise. To the contrary, Jesus taught his disciples that discipleship is a way of suffering that may end in death (Matthew 10:11-25; Luke 9:23-24).

When people of faith experience the pains and struggles of life and are able to deal with them with a sense of calm assurance, trusting in the power of God to work in their lives, it is such a powerful example to others. Many Christians have faced terrible illness in their lives with a sense of peace, confident in God's providence in their lives. Persons of faith who suffer loss and death with assurance and openness to the gift of God's comforting presence provide powerful examples to persons who know only fear in their lives. The history of the church is filled with persons who live their lives knowing that no matter the outcome, they are still in God's hands. They know the love of God will always be with them, even in difficult times. These persons are faithful witnesses to the transforming power of God in Jesus Christ.

Isn't this the message of Advent? In this season when we not only remember the coming of God into the world in the person of Jesus Christ but also anticipate and prepare for Christ's coming again, we affirm that it is God's desire to be among us and to walk with us in the "stuff" of life. God's constant presence with us, God's reaching out to us especially in our times of need, provides hope in the midst of despair and an abiding joy in the midst of sorrow. Persons of faith have an inner peace that enables them to face the turmoil of life with confidence. This faith was made known by Jesus Christ who was born in Bethlehem and laid in a manger, who lived and walked among us, who willingly gave his life so that we might have life.

What difference has Jesus Christ made in your life? Perhaps your ethical behavior has changed. Perhaps there are differences between how you view the world and how others you know view the world. Are the people who know you able to see the difference that your faith makes in your life, or do you keep it well hidden? There used to be a poster that said, "If anyone accused you of being a Christian, would there be enough evidence to convict?" It's a good question for us to reflect upon, especially in this time when so little distinguishes the daily life of the Christian from the person who does not follow Christ.

How has following Christ changed you? Are these changes visible to others? What are marks of the Christian faith that others will recognize?

THE SIGNS OF THE HEART
Matthew 11:2-11

What evidence demonstrated that Jesus of Nazareth was the chosen one of God, anointed to bring the good news to all the people? John the Baptist wanted to know; but before he could receive an answer, Herod Antipas had him imprisoned for daring to speak the harsh truth about him. John sent some of his followers to Jesus to ask, "Are you the one, or should we expect someone else?" Earlier, while he was still baptizing persons in the Jordan River, John had proclaimed that there was one coming who would baptize with fire and the Holy Spirit. Obviously, John had some firm beliefs about who the messiah should be and what the messiah should do. When Jesus came to be baptized, John recognized Jesus as the chosen one; and out of a sense of unworthiness, he tried to prevent Jesus from being baptized (Matthew 3:14-15).

John sent disciples to Jesus, which demonstrates that doubt and uncertainty had crept into his mind. Perhaps Jesus had not lived up to expectations that John had for the Messiah. John may have been looking for more dramatic evidence than Jesus had presented. He may have expected Jesus to free him from prison. The Scriptures do not really tell us why John had these questions.

Jesus answered John's questions by pointing to his actions: The blind now see, the deaf hear, and the lame walk. The dead are raised, and the poor receive good news. Wasn't this evidence enough? Hadn't John seen and heard the evidence himself?

Jesus was not just listing his accomplishments. Jesus was reminding John of the prophetic word of Isaiah, who said that one was coming who would heal the sick and bring good news to the poor. He was telling John not just that he had done wonderful works, but that he had fulfilled the prophecies of the Hebrew Scriptures. Indirectly Jesus was telling John that, yes, he was the Messiah; however, he would not be the kind of messiah that John was expecting.

If John wanted an answer to his question, he only had to look at the actions of Jesus, and then remember that this is what God had promised, even though this did not meet popular expectations of the day.

If Jesus is indeed the Messiah, then what can we say about John the Baptist? Many had gone to the wilderness to be baptized by him, to hear his message of repentance and the coming of a new kingdom. Some who heard Jesus' response may have doubted that he was the messiah, and some may well have believed that John had given them false hope for a coming kingdom.

Jesus asked the disciples of John why they had gone out to the wilderness. Had they gone to see the reeds that grow along the banks of the Jordan? Did they go out to see someone who was well-connected and rich and had much to gain by maintaining the status quo? Jesus affirms for them that John was indeed a prophet, one who pointed them to his coming. John was the last of God's prophets. Jesus had come to initiate a new kingdom and a new way of being. Exactly what Jesus meant by stating that the least in the kingdom of heaven is greater than John is somewhat ambiguous. Would this great prophet of God be excluded from the Kingdom simply because of timing? Or is Jesus' statement based on John's apparent uncertainty about who Jesus is?

Many believe that there must be empirical evidence that demonstrates that Jesus is God's chosen Messiah, the Savior of the world. John seems to have been among those who wanted or needed to see the proof. Christians today often approach the good news of Jesus Christ like an attorney seeking to prove her or his case with a convincing list of evidence. The problem with this is that even if scientific evidence could demonstrate that Jesus is the Messiah, a person's heart still needs to be changed. Repentance is still essential, for Christians are people of faith more than they are people of evidence. Sharing the good news means entering into the life-changing experience of the love of God in Jesus Christ.

Many churches experience an increase in attendance as Christmas approaches. The "holly and the lily" crowd sometimes angers the faithful, every-week churchgoers when the holiday worshipers take up all the space in the parking lot and sit in their favorite pews in the back of the church. Their presence may even require persons to share a weekly bulletin or hymnal. This is sad, for Advent is one of the best seasons of the year to invite people to church. The more commercialized Christmas becomes, the greater becomes the hunger within those who have bought into its commercialized offerings. Now is a perfect time to proclaim the good news that Jesus offers the healing and wholeness to all people. "Are you the one?" is not an uncommon question.

The best evidence, however, is not found in miracles and healings. It is found in the changed hearts of faithful Christians who have experienced the love of Jesus Christ and live their lives in the knowledge and love of God. There is a great transforming power in the story of a heart changed by Jesus Christ. We need to share the story of how our hearts have been changed, to tell the world how Jesus Christ has made a difference. When faithful people can demonstrate that they are different because Jesus Christ has come into their lives, that will be the evidence, the sign that Jesus is the true Messiah. In our world today, we are God's signs made new in the power of Jesus Christ.

For some, the transformation is dramatic. Some overcome addictions. Others turn from patterns and behaviors that are destructive or addictive. The transformation that God works in human lives takes many forms. When confronted by actions that others are ready to condemn, they are ready to forgive. When others are filled with hate and rage, they are filled with compassion and love. When others are unsatisfied with their occupations because others seem to be "more successful," they count success not by their job title or the size of their paycheck, but by the many friendships they have formed or by the help they have been able to offer to those in need.

Identifying how Jesus Christ has made a difference in your life is invaluable as you prepare to share the good news with others. Our preparation for Christmas becomes more satisfying when we look deeply within ourselves and discover the many ways in which Jesus Christ has transformed us.

What reasons would you give for why Jesus Christ came into the world? What evidence would you cite to someone who asked you about your faith in Jesus Christ?

SIGNS OF TRANSFORMATION

Signs of the Savior

Scriptures for Advent: The Fourth Sunday
Isaiah 7:10-16
Romans 1:1-7
Matthew 1:18-25

Before leaving for a road trip, we prepare by gathering information about where we are going. For example, we include maps, because maps help us navigate our journey. However, maps are not enough by themselves. As we travel, we look for signs along the way that will confirm what we see on a map, such as signs with road numbers, exit signs, or signs with street names. Signs not only give us direction, they confirm that we are on the right path.

We also need signs when we talk about our spiritual journey, moving closer and closer to God through Jesus Christ. How do we know that the direction that we are going is the way God wants us to travel? We look for signs of affirmation or assurance, signs of God's presence in our journey.

The biblical story is filled with signs. Some appear in nature, some take the form of historical events, and some appear in the form of people who respond to God's call.

Prophets, apostles, and ordinary people are among signs God offers to a world seeking a savior. Their faithfulness to God demonstrates confidence and assurance. Their willingness to stand up faithfully in the midst of adversity is a sign of the steadfast presence of God. These persons were God's witnesses for those seeking hope in their lives.

Christians anticipating the return of Christ need signs, too. At the same time, we must as faithful people be signs for all those seeking truth and meaning in their lives. Advent is a time for Christians to ask, "How can I be a sign of Jesus Christ in my world? How can I demonstrate that Jesus Christ is the hope of the world?" Does our celebration of the birth of the Savior point others to the gift of grace that God offers us, or does it send mixed messages?

When we are this close to Christmas, many people begin to check their lists to make sure that everything has been done, that all the gifts have been purchased, and that all the greeting cards have been sent. Christians need to check the list of their lives, too, in order to reflect on their relationship with Jesus Christ. This is the time to make sure that we know the meaning of the season for our lives and the significance of the birth of Jesus for the world.

GOD WILL GIVE US SIGNS
Isaiah 7:10-16

When God speaks, do we listen? Most faithful people will say that of course they listen to God; however, there is often some kind of bargaining going on. "I hear you Lord, but I don't see it that way. I think we should do this..."

God offered Ahaz, the king of Judah from approximately 735–715 B.C., the opportunity to ask for a divine sign. Ahaz, however, refused to ask for a sign, claiming that he was unwilling to put God to the test. If that were all we knew about Ahaz, we might conclude that he was a very faithful king. In 2 Chronicles 28:19, however, we learn that Ahaz was actually a faithless king who time and again severely tested God. For example, instead of standing with the kings of Israel and Sytria, Ahaz sought to make an alliance with the Assyrian king. He adopted some of the religious practices of Assyria, turning away from the worship of the one true God. Despite his faithful sounding words, Ahaz did not have faith in God.

Through the prophet Isaiah, God responded to the king, "Is it too little for you to weary mortals, that you weary my God also?" (Isaiah 7:13). God was not pleased with Ahaz's supposed piety, so God decided to send the sign for which Ahaz refused to ask. God would not be silenced by the king's refusal. The sign would be a child born to a young woman. The name of the child would be *Immanuel*, "God is with us." Given the alliance that Ahaz was seeking to make with the Assyrian power, the name of the child was a reminder that God would continue to stand with the people of Judah. In God alone should the king and his people trust, for the powers of other kingdoms could not compare with the power of God.

From the beginning of the church, Christians have traditionally read this passage as a prophecy of the virgin birth. However, the original Hebrew word, *'almah,* means a "young woman." It does not imply that the woman was a virgin. Why, then, does Matthew 1:23 quote this verse and state explicitly that "the virgin shall conceive"?

The Hebrew Scriptures were translated into Greek about 200 B.C. This Greek version of the Hebrew Scriptures, known as the Septuagint, was widely used in the first century A.D. by both Jews and Christians. In this version, the word *parthenos* was used to translate *'almah. Parthenos* means "young woman," but it also can refer to a virgin. When the early church, learning the story of

Jesus, began reading the Hebrew Scriptures to look for signs of Christ (a method Jesus himself seemed to authorize in Luke 24:44-45), they saw the word *parthenos* as a sign of Mary's virginity and thus believed the text of the prophecy was fulfilled in Jesus. When we limit the discussion to the time of Ahaz, however, it is uncertain who the young woman is. Perhaps it is the prophet's wife, or perhaps it is the daughter of King Ahaz. Either way, the child who was to be born would be known to the king and to the prophet. It is not the identity of the child that is important, however. What is important is that the child would be a sign from God.

Isaiah then explained how the child would be a sign. Before this child was old enough to choose between good and evil—in other words, very shortly—Israel and Syria would fall to the Assyrians and no longer be a threat to Judah. The king needed to realize that God was the only ally that the people of Judah needed. God was with them and this child would be the sign. They sought alliances elsewhere, however. The Assyrian army that would crush their neighbors to the north would do the same to them. There was no need for alliances with the Assyrians, or any other power, to provide protection for the people of Judah. God was their fortress and their foundation. All their hopes could rest on God.

Many of the prophets used signs to share the word of God. Isaiah and Hosea gave their children names that were signs to the people (Isaiah 7:1; Hosea 1:2-8). Amos used the sign of a plumb line (Amos 7:7-9). Jeremiah had the sign of the yoke (Jeremiah 27:2). Ezekiel spoke of signs, actually calling himself and his actions signs for the people of Jerusalem (Ezekiel 4; 12). Signs are a visible means of communicating the word of God. The prophets often had difficult messages to deliver. Their messages were about serious matters, and they needed a means to get the attention of the people. They used signs as a way of pointing the people toward the future that was to come. At some time in the future, the people would remember the prophetic message contained in the signs.

God continues to surround us with signs today: signs of God's presence and love, signs of warning, and signs of hope. A newborn baby or the first crocus that pushes its way up through the snow are signs that life is renewing and continuing. The light of a candle burning in the darkness is a sign of God's hope that overcomes the darkness of despair. The face of a starving child that looks at us through the pages of a magazine or through the television screen is a sign that all is not well in the family of God and stands as a warning that we are still called to reach out to the least and the lost of our world.

This week the fourth candle is lit on the Advent wreath. It is a prominent sign to the church that our expectant waiting for the return of Christ is almost complete. The time has almost arrived for the church to celebrate the birth of Christ, the greatest sign of God's love. Isaiah was not predicting the birth of Jesus; still, the Gospel writer was right to see the words of the prophet as a sign that was fulfilled by Christ. God sent a great sign to the entire world: God is with us. With the birth of Jesus, God was with us. In this way, the meaning of Isaiah's prophecy was broadened in a way that now applies to all generations.

Anticipating and preparing for the coming of the Savior is the focus for the season of Advent. There are signs that God guides us and that God is present with us. There are signs that the world still needs Christ and that Christ will come again. The signs remind us of God's promises. We need to open our eyes to see the signs all around us so that we may receive the great blessings of God.

What are the signs that you have seen that God is active in the world today? Why do we need signs of God's presence? How do these signs help us to grow in our knowledge and love of God through Jesus Christ?

A SIGN OF WHAT?
Romans 1:1-7

"Grace to you and peace from God our Father and the Lord Jesus Christ." This greeting is used in all 13 of the letters written by or attributed to the apostle Paul. They are words that are often passed over quickly as little more than a salutation, but the message is central to Paul's understanding of the gospel. Why did Jesus Christ come into the world? Christ came so that the grace of God might be realized. Grace summarizes the good news of God's saving action through Jesus Christ. Grace is the untethered gift of inclusion in the family of God due to God's steadfast and boundless love.

If grace is the gift, peace is the result. Accepting the gift of grace and affirming the wholeness that God intends for us, makes our hearts right with God and neighbor. The gifts of grace and peace are fulfilled in Jesus Christ. Grace and peace are words of salvation, a word related to healing and wholeness. To be saved is to be delivered from all that leads us away from God. It is a healing of the relationship between God and ourselves that has been broken by sin. This healing is made possible by God's reaching out to humanity in Jesus Christ. Paul, therefore, begins all his letters with this proclamation that salvation is from God alone through our Lord and Savior Jesus Christ, and the effect of that great gift is peace. The salutation that we quickly read over is really a central proclamation of the good news that Paul is sharing with the church.

In these opening verses, Paul tells the Romans that he is set aside to share the good news of Jesus Christ; and this provides the definition of his ministry and his life. He identifies himself in two ways: as an apostle and as a servant. An apostle is one who is sent out. Paul understands his reception of the good news as a commission to share the good news, to be a sign and a witness to the Gentiles. We know from his letters and the Acts of the Apostles that Paul was often in danger as he traveled throughout the Roman Empire preaching the gospel. He was beaten and imprisoned. His life was threatened. His preaching and teaching in the synagogues was rejected. Some Jewish Christians seriously challenged him about his mission to the Gentiles. Paul, however, persevered in spite of his difficulties. He did so because he had a firm foundation in Jesus Christ, and he knew the saving power of Christ in his life.

Paul also describes himself as a servant, which can also be translated as slave. This defines how he views himself in relationship to Christ: Paul willingly gave up his entire life to put himself completely under the lordship of Christ. He surrendered his entire being into the hands of God that he might be used in whatever way God saw fit. Paul's wholehearted trust in God provides a powerful witness to the Romans as it did to all the churches that he helped to form.

It might seem difficult to imagine someone so willing to give of himself as Paul did; however, he goes on to explain how the gospel of which he is servant and apostle was "promised beforehand." The good news of Jesus Christ is part of God's long plan of salvation, spoken of in the words of the prophets and promised in the Davidic covenant. Paul knew that the promises of God were steadfast and true. Through Jesus' coming into the world and through his death and resurrection, God laid claim on the lives of all who will follow. All are "called to belong to Jesus Christ" (verse 6).

Why is this passage included in the readings for the season of Advent, a season of preparation? Paul is not addressing the birth of Jesus or the second coming of Christ. What he is addressing is our spiritual preparation as Christians. Paul understands who he is and whose he is. He understands fully who God wants him to be and that he can be a powerful witness for the gospel because he knows its meaning in his life. It is important that Christians know more than the fact that Jesus is "the reason for the season." Faithful followers of Jesus Christ need to understand how Christ's birth is a gift of grace and makes a difference in their lives. The grace and peace that Paul speaks of with such confidence needs to be understood in real and practical terms.

So what does grace look like? It is the assurance of God's love for those who will have an empty chair at the table this Christmas season.

As joyful as the holiday is, for some it is also one of the loneliest times of the year. Grace is experienced when a faithful follower of Jesus Christ is led to reach out to offer friendship and support to one who is struggling. Grace is the joy a child feels when she learns to sing "Away in the Manger" for the first time; and the look on her face tells you that she not only knows the song, she knows the Savior. Why are these examples of grace? They are examples of grace because they are gifts given freely so that we might grow in our relationship to God, that we might offer ourselves in thanksgiving to God for all we have and all we are. When we are able to grow in our relationship with God through Jesus Christ, we experience peace. We set aside the hectic pace of the holidays and approach the weeks of advent as an opportunity to practice the sabbath rest our God provides, and we are blessed with the time to experience the true peace of the season.

The Advent season is a time for us to reaffirm our faith in Christ, to know the joy of our faith, to remember the powerful love that God has for us. This is the perfect time, when so many others try to locate the meaning of this season in fond memories that are little more than nostalgia, to witness to the power of Jesus Christ. How do we do this? By making worship a priority and by inviting others to worship with us even though there are many other things that we might do with our time. We provide an example of God's grace when we are willing to seek and offer forgiveness and to be made right with others, especially on those occasions when we are uncertain of how the other persons will respond.

We show the meaning of Jesus Christ in our lives when we spend these days of Advent looking for Christ and readying our hearts and minds for our Lord. Instead of collapsing with fatigue the day after Christmas, we will be spiritually prepared to enter fully into the joy of the coming year, ready to receive the grace that has come to us in Jesus Christ.

What difference are these weeks of expectant waiting making in your life? Will there be any difference this year? How have you experienced God's unconditional love that is extended to you generously and freely? How can you point to these experiences of grace as a sign of God's presence in the world today, so that all might be able to experience the power of Jesus Christ in their lives?

SEEING GOD'S SIGNS IN OTHERS
Matthew 1:18-25

Prophets, apostles, and Gospel writers all knew that God had a plan. The story of Jesus Christ did not happen by mere chance. God chose two people who were highly unlikely servants. Mary and Joseph were ordinary people from an ordinary town. They were not powerful. They had no authority. They were not royalty. They did not belong to the priestly caste. Though not married, Joseph and Mary were betrothed, which was a binding marital agreement made between fathers or families. It was considered the first step in marriage, although, the couple would not live together under the same roof until they were married. The laws governing marriage, laws found in the Torah, applied also to a betrothal.

In Matthew, Mary's pregnancy created a dilemma for Joseph, who is the central character in this portion of the Gospel. Knowing that he was not the biological father, his assumption was that her child was another man's, which means that Mary would have committed fornication, possibly adultery. He was in the position of deciding Mary's fate. Leviticus 20:10 calls for a person who has committed adultery to be put to death. Numbers 5 contains a detailed description of a ritual sacrifice that a woman accused of adultery could undergo to be proven innocent; but even if she were proven innocent, she would have been subjected to public disgrace. However, Matthew reminds us that Joseph was a righteous man. He wanted to do the right thing. He resolved to divorce Mary quietly and to release her from her vows of betrothal.

Joseph's desire to do what is right indicates his willingness to trust the word of God that comes from an angel of the Lord in a dream. When God spoke to him, he listened and obeyed, even though it might result in embarrassment for him. The message that he received would be difficult for most people to believe. Only a person of faith who trusts fully in the power of God would dare to believe that Mary's baby was the child of the Holy Spirit. Even the prophecy from Isaiah 7:14 does not mention that the conception of Immanuel will be from the Holy Spirit.

The angel also told Joseph that he was to receive this child as his own. One indication is the naming process. The angel said, "You are to name him Jesus." The honor of naming a child was given to the father. For Joseph to name this child would mean that Joseph would see this child as his own. God obviously had a plan for Joseph. He is not an insignificant bystander in the life of Jesus.

Jesus, the name to be given the child, is the Greek version of the Hebrew name *Joshua*. In the history of the Hebrew people, Joshua was the successor to Moses. It was Joshua who led the people of Israel into the Promised Land after the death of the lawgiver in the mountains of Moab. The name means "YHWH is salvation." The child who is to come will be the salvation of Israel, sent by God. He comes into the world to inaugurate a new kingdom and to lead his followers into a new promised land. Like Joshua, Jesus is the successor of the lawgiver and the fulfillment of the Law itself. The name of Jesus is not arbitrary, coincidental, or insignificant; it is a sign in and of itself.

Any message received in a dream could easily be dismissed as fantasy, but Joseph did not ignore this dramatic word of God. The Scripture tells us that when he awoke, he did what the angel of the Lord told him to do. In biblical times, visions and dreams were viewed with far more seriousness than they are today. There is, however, no indication that there was any fear in Joseph's mind. He listened to the dream and fulfilled his betrothal vows.

Matthew understands the birth of Jesus as a fulfillment of the prophecy of Isaiah. He will be Emmanuel, which means God is with us. Throughout the Gospel, Matthew demonstrates how Jesus Christ is the fulfillment of the Hebrew Scriptures, the messiah spoken of in the prophets, the successor to the Torah. In Jesus, God is no longer sending messengers and the Law; God is actually coming into the midst of the people. This is demonstrated by the birth of Jesus to an ordinary couple who have no place of honor or distinction.

With Joseph and Mary, God provided a home of self-giving love for Jesus. Mary and Joseph were people willing to risk themselves and their honor to fulfill God's plan in the world. Joseph's willingness to do as the angel of the Lord commanded demonstrates that he actively chose to do the will of God, even though he could have opted out.

Joseph's story is a sign for Christians of selfless giving, of offering oneself to God for God's plan. Joseph did not let his ego get in the way. He was willing to take Jesus into his home and into his life, to father the boy that he knew was not his biological child. Even before God's angel appeared to him in a dream, Joseph was a man who wanted to do what was right, to be compassionate when he could have been vengeful, to follow the law but not to bring disgrace upon Mary. Joseph did not seek to do the right thing merely because of good personal feelings towards Mary; rather, his actions evolved from his righteous character and his willingness to trust God. Though not stated within the Gospels, it is easy to see that as Jesus was growing up he had a fine example in his earthly father.

We also see in Joseph a man who heard God's word and listened. Although God calls many of us to serve in our world, we are often reluctant to respond. The timing might not seem right, the situation might appear to be too difficult, or the ministry to which we are called might seem too frightening. God, however, does not call us into any place of service where we will be alone. In Jesus Christ, God is with us, which includes walking with us in our ministry to others.

This is the time to examine our hearts and minds, to know why we are celebrating the birth of Jesus Christ this year, and to know what difference Jesus Christ makes for us. Maybe this will be the best celebration of Christmas yet for you because you have taken the time to be truly ready. What joy that will be for you!

As you reflect on the different people who were instrumental in the story of Christ's birth, what qualities of faith and character stand out to you? How can you emulate these in your life? What does it mean to you to know that God is with you? How do you share that with others?

The Faithful Response

Scriptures for Christmas Eve:
Isaiah 9:2-7
Titus 2:11-14
Luke 2:1-20

No Christmas Eve service would be complete without the singing of carols. Something stirs in our hearts as our congregation sings "O Come, All Ye Faithful" or "Joy to the World." There is a peace that comes upon us when the words and music of "It Came Upon the Midnight Clear," "O Little Town of Bethlehem," or "Silent Night" fill the church. Music creates an intuitive response, but the message of the carols does even more. As we sing the old, old story of the birth of Jesus, the message becomes more than a 2,000-year-old story. It becomes our story. We experience the joy that comes in the Savior, and we feel the heavenly peace that surrounds and holds us. We feel the triumph of God's saving grace alongside the still, small voice that speaks to our innermost selves.

The birth of the Savior is a remarkable event that changed the world. It is so extraordinary that a person of faith cannot help but respond, and the celebration of Christmas provides many opportunities to respond. God has always called on people of faith to respond to the great gift of grace. Isaiah's prophecies, though at times difficult to hear, also celebrated the deliverance that God would bring to the people. God's continual reaching out to the world evokes great joy and hope.

The pastoral epistles ask people of faith to respond to the good news of God's grace in their lives. Paul reminds the people in the churches he formed to live transparent lives that would demonstrate their response to God's grace in Jesus Christ. In so doing, they would bring the good news to others. The story of the birth of Jesus evokes a response in faithful followers who cannot help but hear the story again and again with a sense of awe and joy. As we read the story, we find that many of our own responses are similar to those of the shepherds and Mary.

The birth of Jesus is the birth of a Savior, news that is too good to be kept from others. We must proclaim the joy of this celebration!

LIGHT IN THE DARKNESS
Isaiah 9:2-7

The announcement of the birth of a child is usually a moment of great joy. When that child is of royal heritage, the announcement is surrounded by great fanfare and ceremony. For the people of Jerusalem, the birth of a royal child carried with it the affirmation of God's continuing loyalty to the covenant with the chosen people. In the time of Isaiah, the people of Jerusalem were looking to their neighbors to the north who were under attack by the Assyrian army and struggling for their survival. Would Jerusalem be next? Had God forgotten the covenant with the chosen people? It was a dark and difficult time, as the people lived in fear of a similar fate.

With the announcement of the birth of a child, a new generation of royalty, there was hope that there would be future generations, that the Davidic line of succession would continue, and that the covenant with God was still active and intact. Isaiah 9:2-7 is a hymn of thanksgiving in celebration of the birth of child, a new king. Some scholars have viewed this as a coronation hymn, particularly because of the titles that appear within it. The verses, however, state that "a child has been born for us, a son given to us" (verse 6). The event being celebrated is the birth of a child, not the coronation of a new king.

Why would this child be so important for the people of Jerusalem? The prophetic song explains. The previous chapters of Isaiah describe dark days for the people, and the prophetic message conveys little hope. The Assyrian army will sweep into Judah, and the invasion will be swift and harsh. This, however, will not be the ruin of the nation, for the prophet says that in the midst of their darkness a light will shine. Joy will fill the nation. The advancing army will not bring defeat and oppression upon the people of Judah. The child of this song of thanksgiving will be their salvation. He will be their ruler, and will establish peace and security for the people of Judah.

Although the child mentioned in this poem is often believed to be Hezekiah, no specific evidence exists within the text to indicate this. What is clear is that the Scripture presents the ruler as a sign of hope for the people of Judah. The royal titles attributed to him speak of a grandeur greater than what would be expected at the birth of an ordinary child who was not royal. *Wonderful Counselor, Mighty God, Everlasting Father,* and *Prince of Peace* are titles that indicate a ruler who is in a position of great power. No one but a king would have such remarkable titles.

Kingship for the people of Israel was more than a political office. The king embodied the best qualities of the nation. Throughout the history of God's chosen people, the stories of the many kings contain notations about whether he did good or evil in the sight of the Lord. When the king was obedient to the will of God, the people followed suit. When the king was disobedient, the nation likewise followed. People viewed the king and his authority as divine promise and covenant. The four titles used in this prophetic song say something about the king, but they also express the vision for the nation.

The great titles of this passage indicate that this ruler who has been born will be an extraordinarily faithful and wise leader who will guide the people with a gentle hand and a vision for the future. This ruler will have a gift of divine power, and a fatherly love that is never-ending and never-failing. This leader will bring peace to the people and will establish a kingdom of understanding and harmony.

The child who has been born, the future leader of the people of Judah, is described in messianic terms. God has anointed this leader to rise up and lead the people into a new way of being. The expectation, however, was not directed toward a distant future messiah but for one who would rise up in the near future to deliver them from imminent threats.

While Christians tend to read these passages as a prediction of the birth of Jesus, a more immediate meaning existed for those who heard these words in the eighth century B.C. They faced the onslaught of the Assyrian army and possible annihilation. The people needed assurance of God's providential care. More than 100 years later, these words would continue to ring true to the Jews under siege in Jerusalem against the Babylonians who had become the new ruling super power. Still later, imagine the comfort these words would have brought to the people in exile, who longed for their Temple. These were dark days, and the people looked for hope. They trusted in God. They knew that God would not forget them but would send someone to save them.

Centuries later, under the oppression of Roman rule, the people of Judea and Galilee were looking for a new messiah, a ruler who would rise up and bring them salvation. Many thought that this would be a leader in the same mode as the great kings of the past: a military and political leader with divine gifts. God saw that the people were living in spiritual darkness. The leader they needed was one who would lead them into a new light. The prophecy was still true but in a new way in a new context.

Today, Christians look to Jesus, the light of the world, to shine in the darkest corners of their lives, to bring hope in the midst of despair, and to bring life in the midst of death. It is easy to dismiss this song of thanksgiving from Isaiah as nothing more than the prelude to the main event, the birth of Jesus. That would be too bad, because it has always been a part of God's plan to bring light to the darkened world, even when the world was not ready to receive the light. From the creation of the world, when God said, "Let there be light," God has desired that the light shine upon us. In the light, we are able to see God and to discern God's plan for our lives. God wants to be in a right relationship with us so that we might meet God face to face.

We have reached the celebration of Christmas, the celebration of the coming of the light of the world. Our need for the light is as important today as the need for the light was in Isaiah's Jerusalem. The difference is that we believe the great light has already come. It has been shining in the darkness 2,000 years. It still shines in our day with amazing brilliance.

In what areas of your life do you need to invite the light of the world to enter? How does the light of Christ make a difference to you? With whom would you like to share the light of Christ this Christmas season?

A CHILD MAKES A DIFFERENCE
Titus 2:11-14

How should a faithful Christian respond to the gift of God's grace? That is the question that Paul is answering in his letter to Titus, a fellow traveler and coworker of the apostle who had been sent as an emissary to provide help and guidance to churches in the midst of turmoil. Paul's letter offers pastoral guidance and instruction to the church; and though the letter itself is addressed to an individual, it is less a personal letter than a letter for the entire community of faith. Paul writes, "For the grace of God has appeared, bringing salvation to all" (Titus 2:11). The foundation of the Christian faith is that salvation for all has come in the person of Jesus Christ. This great gift of love for the world calls for a response from the faithful, and Paul provides a prescription for that response.

Prior to this section, Paul has written a number of instructions for households. Consistency of faith and action is important, but now Paul addresses the most important reason for faithful living. In verse 11, Paul speaks of salvation to all. In verse 12, he speaks of God's grace providing training for "us." Is God's grace only for an elect few? Not at all! The grace of God that works in the lives of the faithful is not meant to be kept as a personal gift. It is meant to be shared with others in order to lead others to Christ. Faithful Christians live lives that allow the grace that God has given them in Christ to shine through them. Christ coming into the world needs to mean something tangible and visible, a light to the nations, to those who have not yet heard the good news of Jesus Christ. Emmanuel, God with us, calls forth such a response of faith.

Paul lists several ways in which faithful Christians can respond to God's grace in Christ: "Renounce impiety and worldly passions, and in the present age to live lives that are self-controlled, upright, and godly" (verse 12). Christians are being called to be different, to set themselves apart from the kind of world in which they lived. Titus would have known this world well because he was a Gentile Christian. Paul had sent him to Corinth, a major seaport and cosmopolitan center of the Roman Empire. Throughout the Roman Empire, immorality and pagan religious practice were common. Christians had to live differently if they were to be witnesses. Their lifestyles needed to reflect God's grace. Christians would lead others to the saving grace of God through Jesus Christ by living lives that others would want to emulate.

Christ came into the world that the world might be redeemed, rescued from a place of separation from God. This great message of hope is at the heart of the Christian life. The familiar carol "Good Christian Friends, Rejoice" closes with the verse that states: "Now ye need not fear the grave ... / Jesus Christ was born to save!" This was the message that Paul communicated to Titus. It remains a foundational message of hope for the world. Christmas affirms the believer's faith in the saving power of Christ.

Christmas is a great gift of grace that can fill us when we are empty and lift us when we are downtrodden. It assures us that we are never alone, that God is always with us and desires to draw near to us.

In recent years, some churches have begun to hold Blue Christmas services, held just before Christmas on the longest night of the year. This service is designed for those who find the Christmas holidays to be difficult. These are services of hope for those who have lost loved ones and will have an empty place at the table this year, those who have lost their jobs, or those who are far away from family and friends and will spend their holidays alone.

The Longest Night service is actually a celebration of grace, a thanksgiving service that affirms that in the midst of the darkest time of the year, the light of Christ still shines, just as in the darkest places in our lives, the light of Christ continues to shine. Many persons who are not in difficulty also find these services to be profoundly meaningful, for they provide an opportunity to meditate on why Christ came into the world and how God's saving grace has made a difference in their lives.

THE FAITHFUL RESPONSE

We often do not take the opportunity to affirm how the grace of God makes us different. Being different is not necessarily fun; but if we live a life of integrity that is consistent with the gospel, our lives may speak louder than any verbal proclamation that we can make. Many Christians will gather for Christmas candlelight services, light candles, and sing carols. They will listen to a reading of the story of the birth of Christ.

At the same time, we should not forget that as these services are being held, people are hungry and homeless, people are separated from loved ones due to border disputes and war, people are in hospital beds, and people are home alone. Some will see Christmas services as a waste of time that interrupts their busy schedules of parties and other family gatherings. Christ has come for all such persons as well as for us. Christ has come to all who need to experience the grace of God. Our task as Christians is to share how God's grace has lifted us up, how Christ has made a difference for us. When we can show this, we can show the world that Jesus Christ came to save. Paul wrote to Titus, encouraging those to whom he was bringing the message of salvation to let the light of Christ shine in them, so that through them others might know God's grace.

How do you let others know that the grace of God makes a difference for you and for the world? Are your behaviors, actions, and attitudes different because Christ came into the world? Who do you know who needs to experience the gift of God's grace in their lives?

A CHILD IS BORN
Luke 2:1-20

Night had fallen over the town of Bethlehem, a small town just a few miles south of the city of Jerusalem. Joseph and Mary had traveled to Bethlehem to register for the census that had been decreed by the emperor Augustus. We can assume that the town was crowded that night, as the Gospel writer makes the point that there was no room in the inn. It was while they were in Bethlehem that Mary gave birth to her first-born son.

Throughout the centuries, this setting has been idealized, captured in paintings and songs; and many stories and legends have grown out of the account of the birth of Jesus. What gets lost in many of these depictions of the Nativity is the harshness of the circumstances. The city of Bethlehem was over 70 miles from the little village of Nazareth. Travel from Galilee to Judea was difficult and dangerous, requiring travel through the Jordan valley and then up the Jericho Road through the Judean wilderness. Travelers who made this trip did not confuse it with a pleasure outing. Mary was well into her pregnancy, so traveling must have been difficult for her. Exactly what accommodations were available to travelers in Bethlehem is not known. What Luke tells us is that there were no accommodations for Joseph and Mary.

Luke mentions no innkeeper, nor does he mention exactly where the Baby was born. He only states that the Baby was wrapped in bands of cloth (a common practice of the day) and placed in a manger, a feeding trough for the animals. From this, readers have concluded that Jesus was born in a stable with the animals; but this is not specifically mentioned. In fact, since poorer Palestinian Jewish families often kept their animals in a downstairs room of their home at night, Jesus may well have been born in someone's home. All Luke tells us is that Jesus was not born in an inn.

God did not enter our world in the midst of comfort or luxury. God came into our world in an extremely humble manner, without privilege and without fanfare. This fits Luke's image that Jesus came for the least and the last of society. From his birth forward, Jesus identified with the ordinary people of his day. This theme is further enhanced by God's choosing the shepherds to announce the birth of the Messiah.

Even though both David and Moses had been shepherds, respectable Jews considered shepherds to be among the lowest of society. There was no longer anything honorable about being a shepherd. The reader in the first century would picture a worthless, perhaps even dishonest, person with a rough exterior and a harsh interior in sharp contrast to the idealized images that we picture today. God is gathering still more unlikely people around the birth of the Messiah.

In his telling of the birth of Jesus, Luke gives more detail about the shepherds and the angel than he does about the birth itself, which is stated in a straightforward manner without much detail. The angel of the Lord appears, and the glory of the Lord shines upon them. The glory of the Lord is mentioned elsewhere in the Scriptures, and it signifies God's immediate presence. When the glory of the Lord appears to Moses and the Israelites, the word of God comes to them. These angels have come to bring the word of God.

The angel's message is one of "good news of great joy for all the people" (verse 10). Though delivered first to these shepherds on the hillside, the message is intended for all people. The good news is the birth of the messianic Savior in Bethlehem, the city of David. A child can be found wrapped in bands of cloth and lying in a manger. A newborn child is not all that unusual, nor is a child wrapped in bands of cloth; but rarely are newborns placed in a feeding trough. The multitude of angels completes their message by singing a song of praise to God in the highest. The Savior that has been born will bring peace to all the people.

The image of a child lying in a manger is in direct contrast to the opening lines of Luke 2, which name the ruling powers of the day: Caesar Augustus and Quirinius, the governor of Syria. The emperor in Rome was supposed to be the great keeper of the peace. Vast imperial armies that no one would dare to challenge were meant to keep Caesar's subjects in line. Yet, Luke names Jesus as the true Prince of Peace, an image that echoes the prophecies of Isaiah. The true Prince of Peace does not utilize military might but has a humble heart and exercises complete trust in God.

The shepherds' story continued once the angels departed. Even though the angels had not ordered them to seek out this child, the shepherds went to Bethlehem to find this child, the Child who had been born. Their response demonstrates how, even though they were considered less than desirable members of society, they understood the importance of this message. They understood that this was God's word for them and the world. The shepherds became the first evangelists, as they not only found the baby but also shared the good news of great joy that the angel had brought to them.

Luke states that all who heard it were amazed. Whether "all" refers to just Joseph and Mary, or includes others who had gathered, is uncertain. The message of the angels was an amazing revelation to all. This baby, lying in a manger, was the Savior, the Davidic messiah who had been promised for centuries. The words of the angels, the glory of the Lord that surrounded the shepherds, and the angelic choir all affirmed this.

There is one final contrast in this part of the story. Mary, Jesus' mother, pondered all these words about her son in her heart; but the shepherds returned to the hillside glorifying and praising God. Mary and the shepherds had profound responses: One was a quiet reflective response; the other was a joyful response of praise and thanksgiving. Their responses differed, but neither could ignore the birth of Jesus.

By the time Christmas arrives each year, many people have been so busy for weeks that their only response is one of relief. This is a shame, for Christmas Day is the first day of a twelve-day celebration of the Incarnation, God becoming flesh. The season of Christmas begins on Christmas Eve and continues to Epiphany on January 6th. For persons who have been waiting expectantly since the beginning of Advent, Christmas is a time to celebrate that God has come to us. We hear the message with new ears and see the story with new eyes. No matter how familiar we are with the story of the birth of Christ, it will seem amazingly new, because our hearts have been made anew and Christ is speaking to us in new ways.

How do you respond to the good news that Christ the Savior is born? Are you like Mary who is reflective, pondering all this in your heart, gaining quiet comfort and peace? Or are you like the shepherds, excited by the good news, ready to shout it from the mountaintops, outwardly joyful and filled with praise? Your life circumstances at the moment, the realizations to which you have come through your preparation for Christ, will influence the responses that you will have. Your faithful response declares that you are a witness to the good news that the Savior has been born, and it makes a difference in your life and in the lives of others. That is what God asks of people of faith, to witness to the difference Christ has made in their lives.

This wonderful celebration stirs our hearts and moves us to service in the name of Jesus Christ. It is a wonderful story, but it means little to us if the only thing we do is read it over like a tale from long ago. This is a story that took place over 2,000 years ago, but the miracle of Christmas is that its power to renew human life continues to happen as we reflect on Christ's birth during the Christmas season.

As you begin your celebration of Christmas, what difference does Jesus make in your life; and how is your celebration of his birth helping you to express that? What spiritual disciplines, such as prayer, song, worship or Bible study, do you use to help you to experience the news of the Savior's birth?